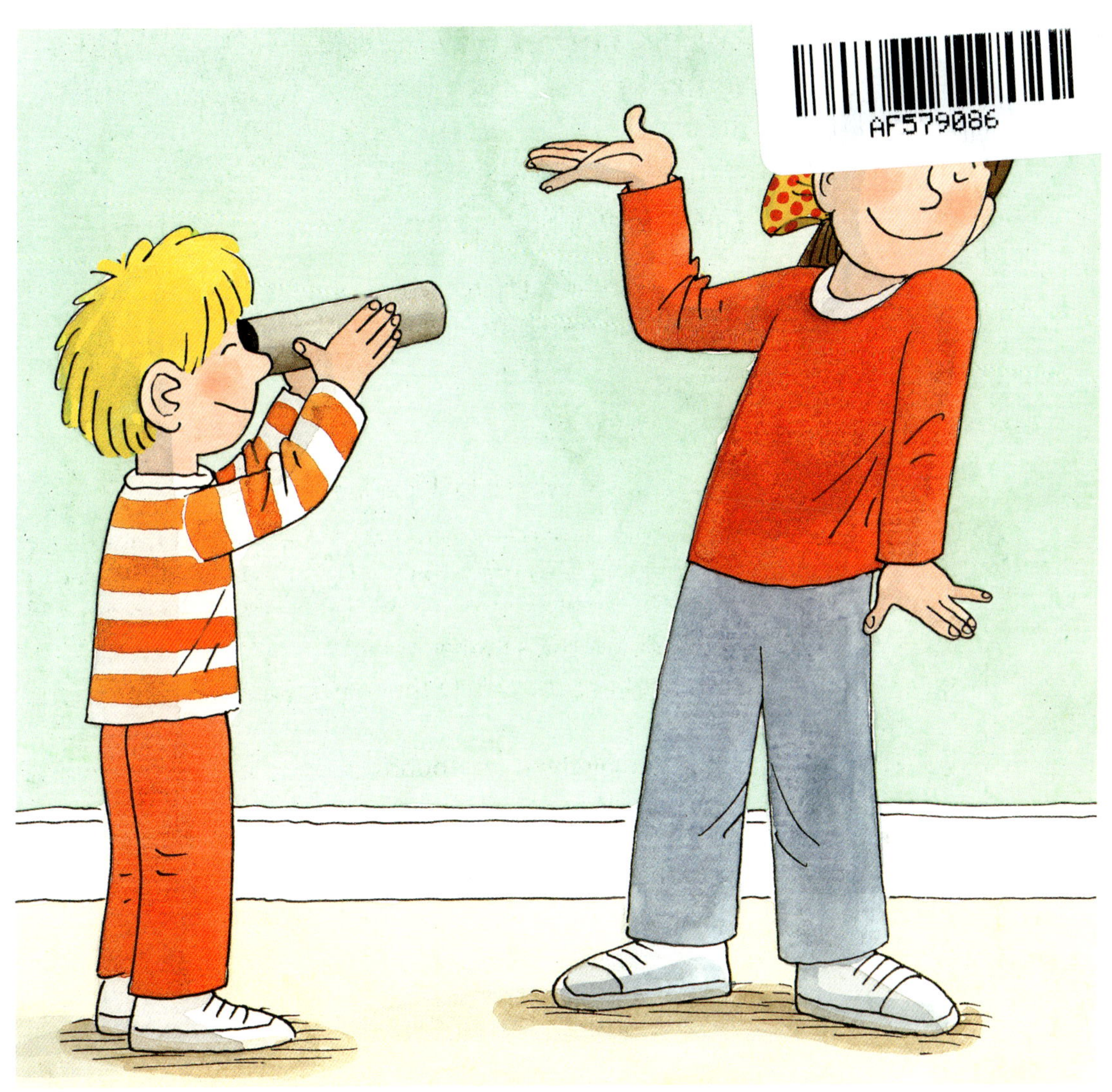

I see Biff.

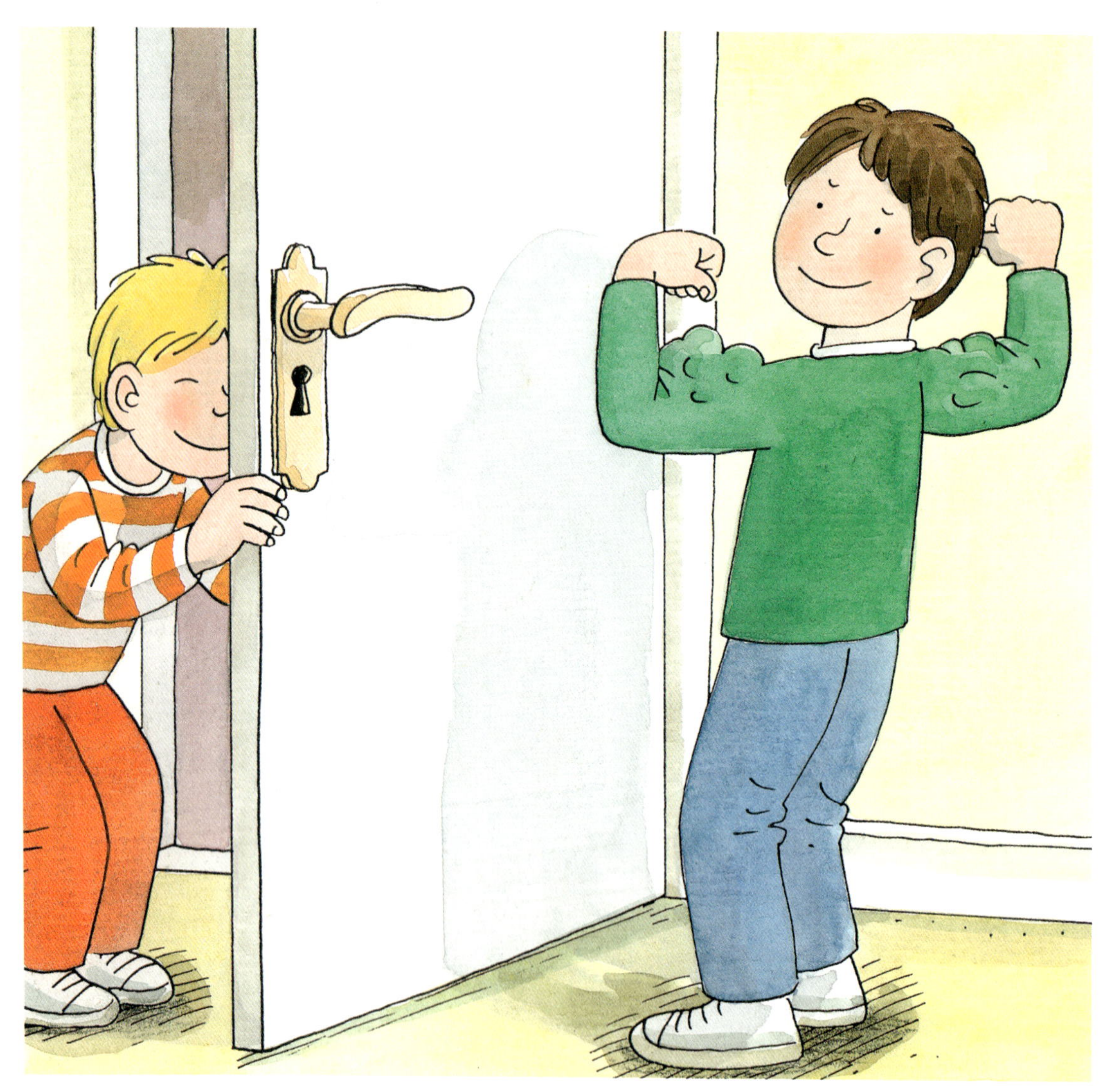

I see Chip.

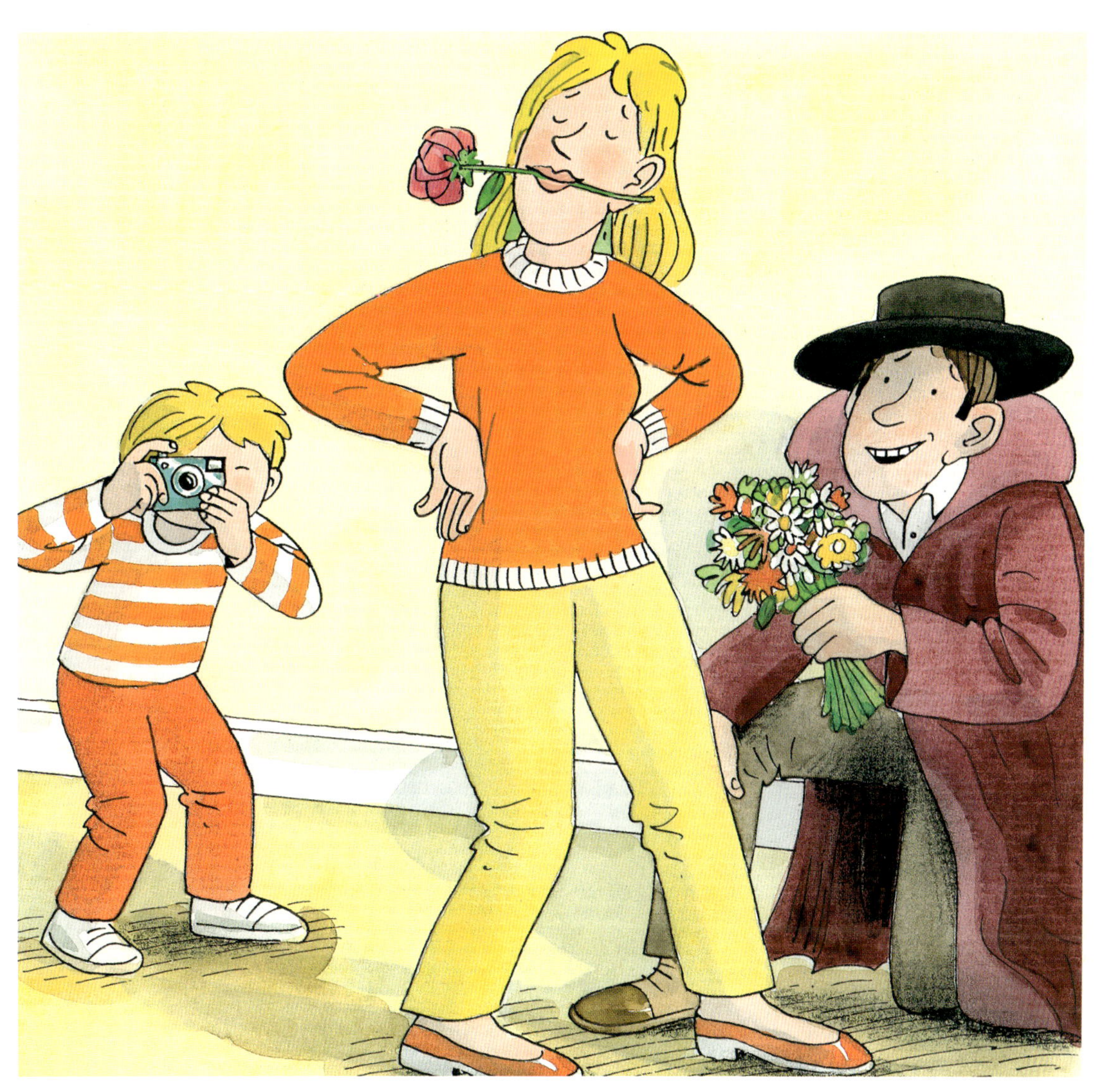

I see Mum and Dad.

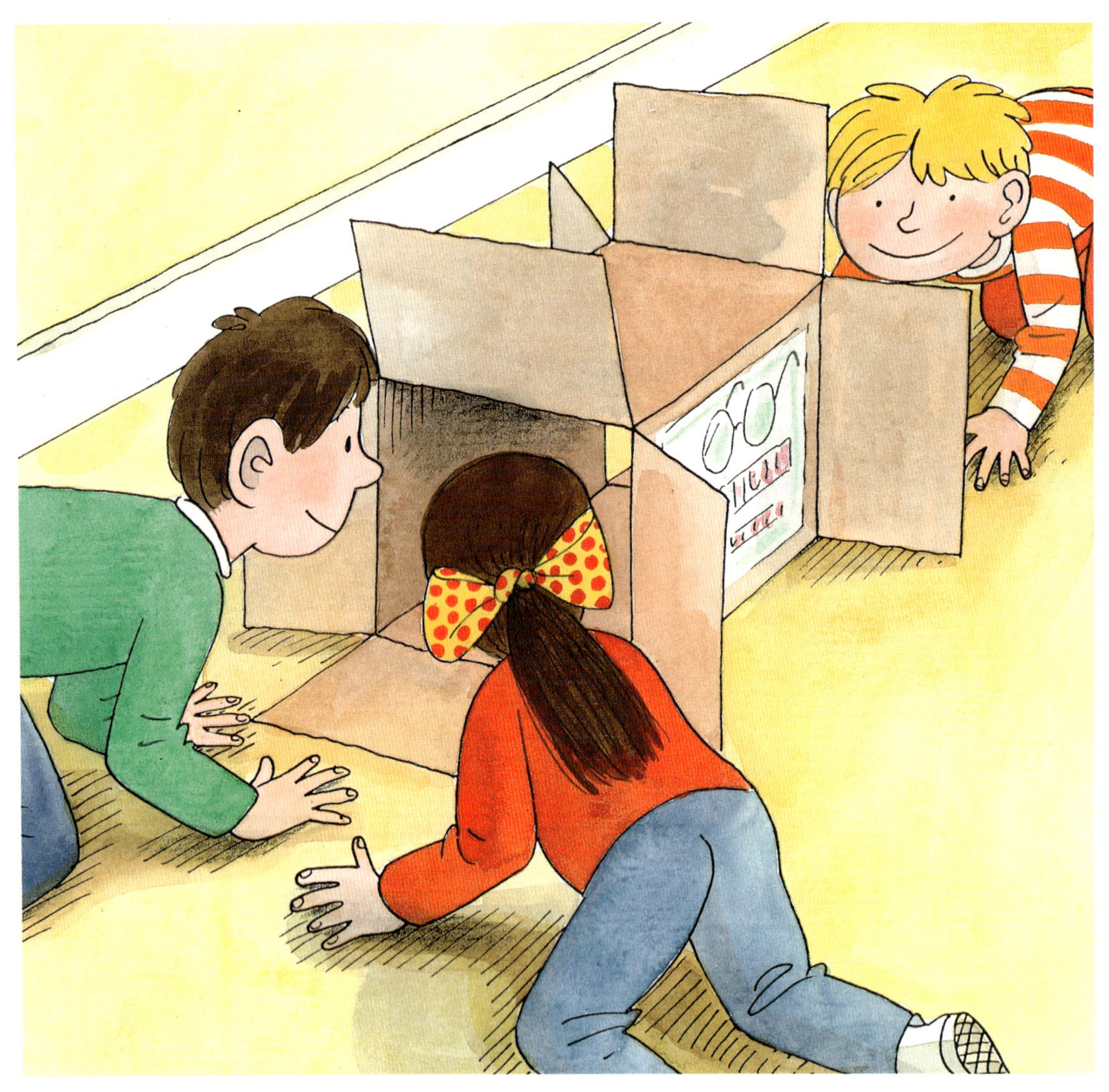

We see Kipper.

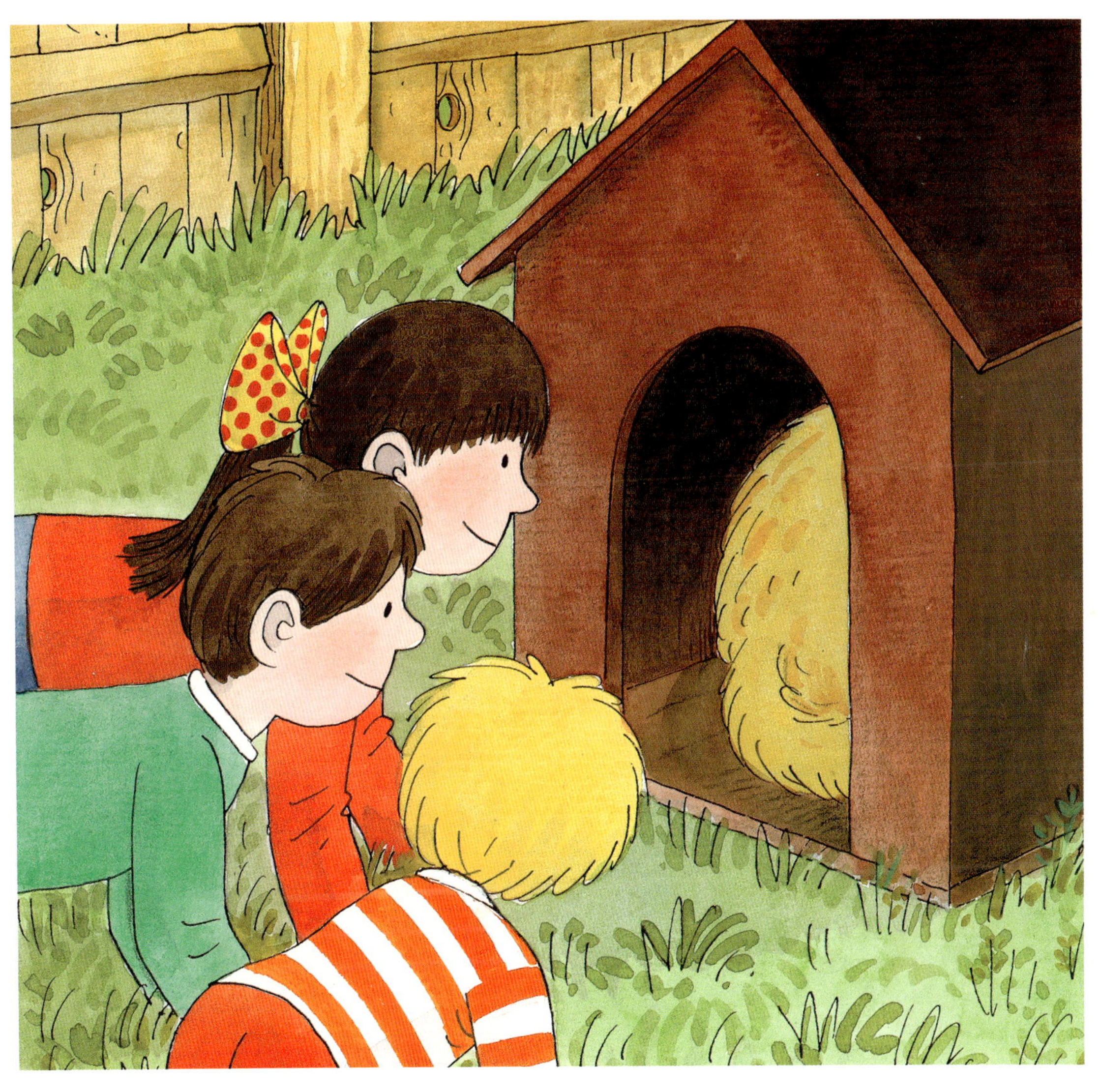

We see Floppy.

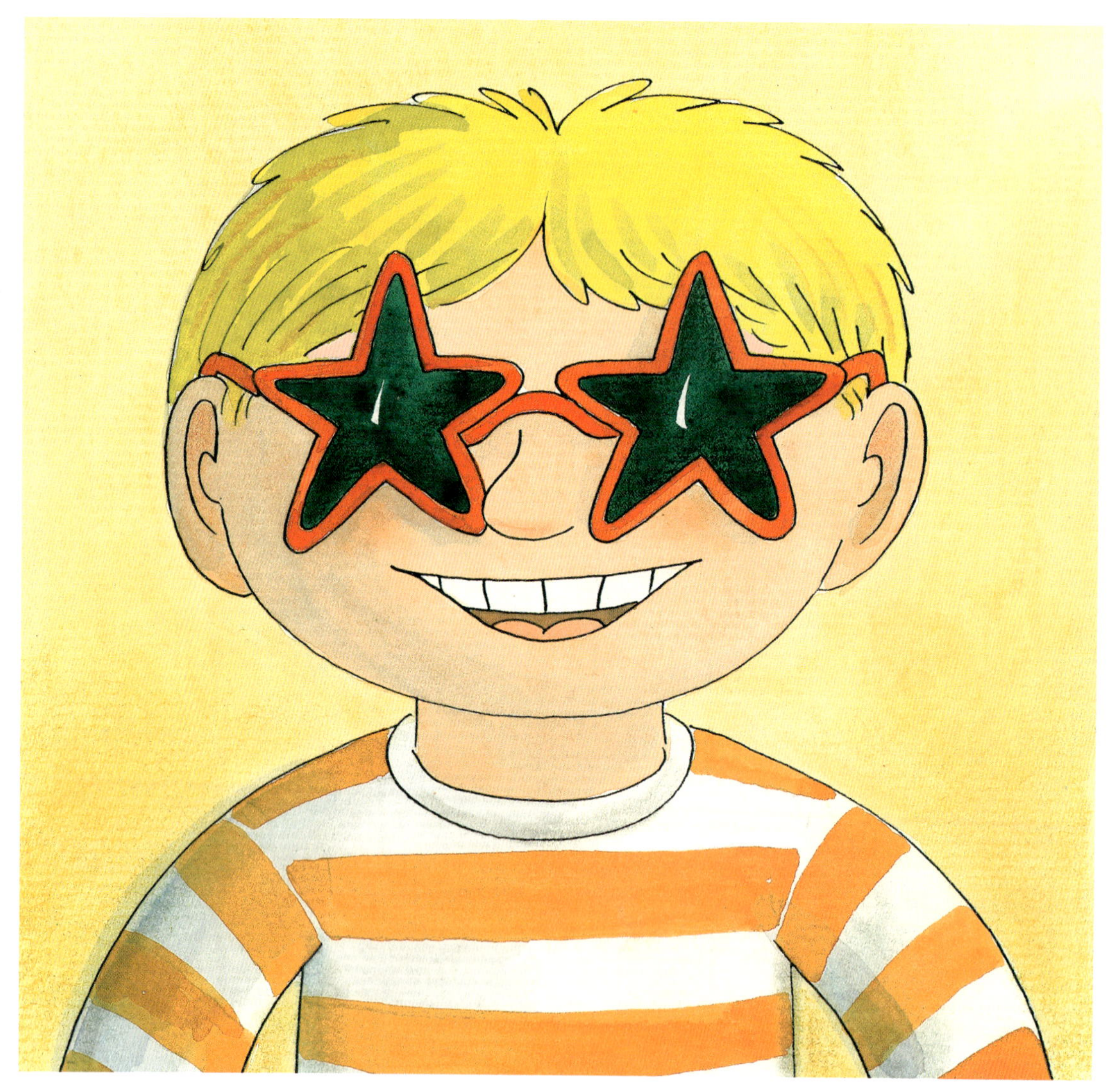

I see Biff and Chip.

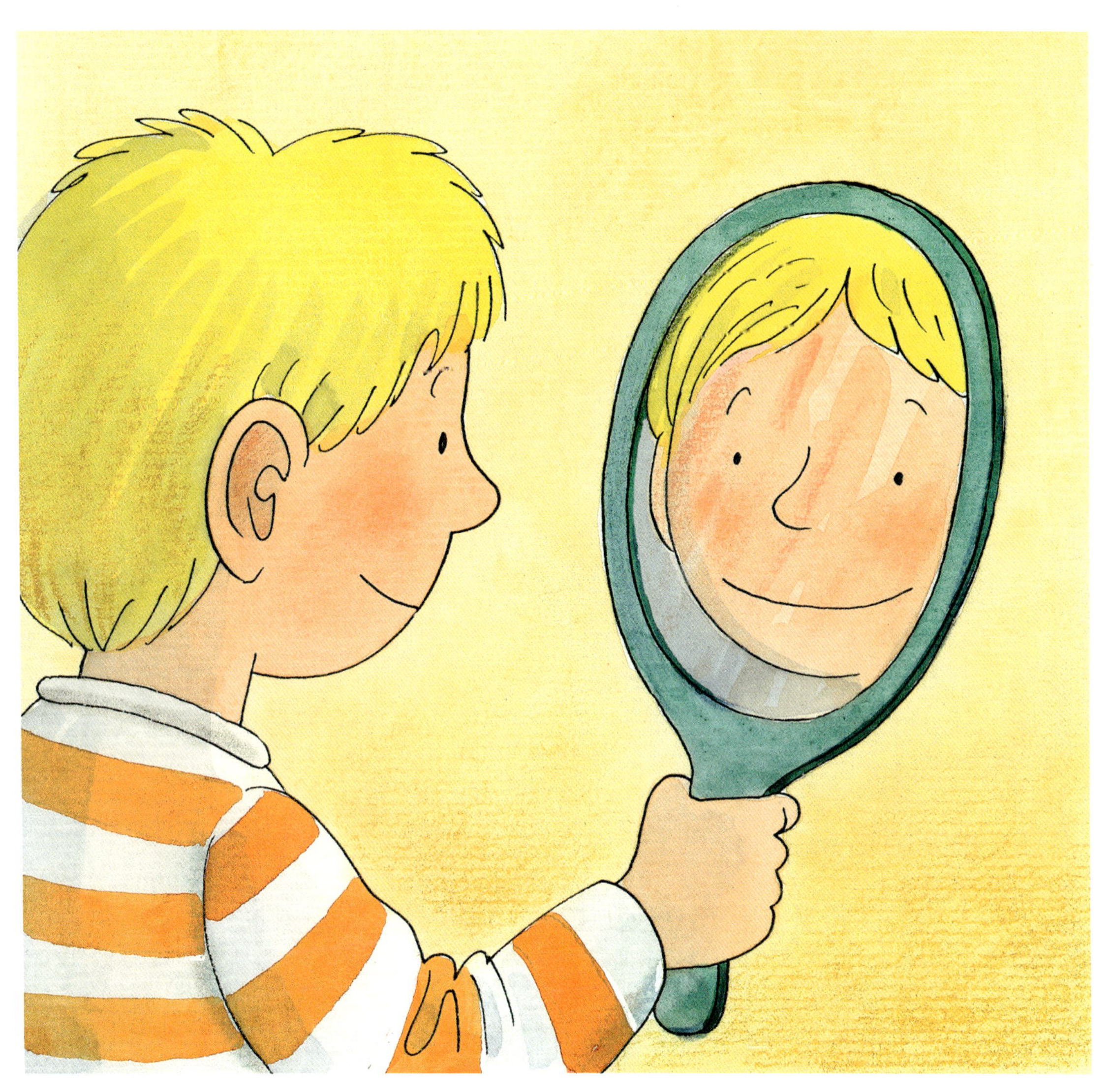

I see me.

Biff

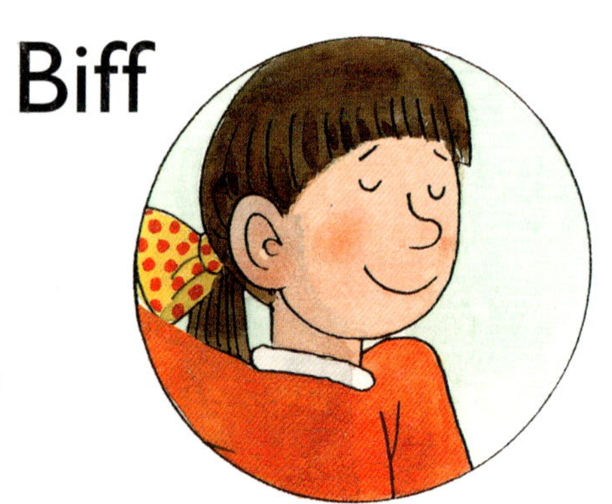

Chip

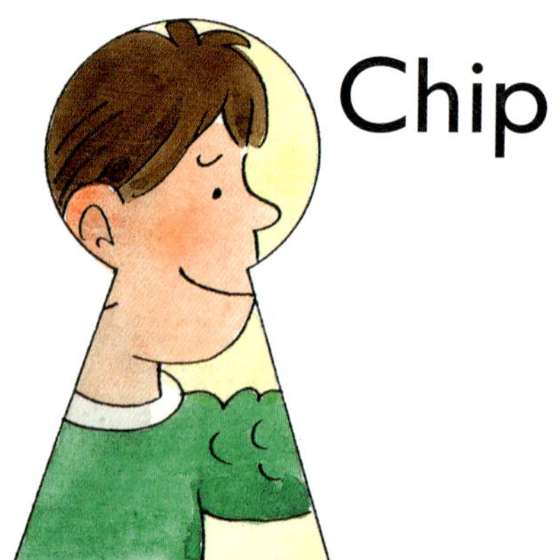

Mum and Dad

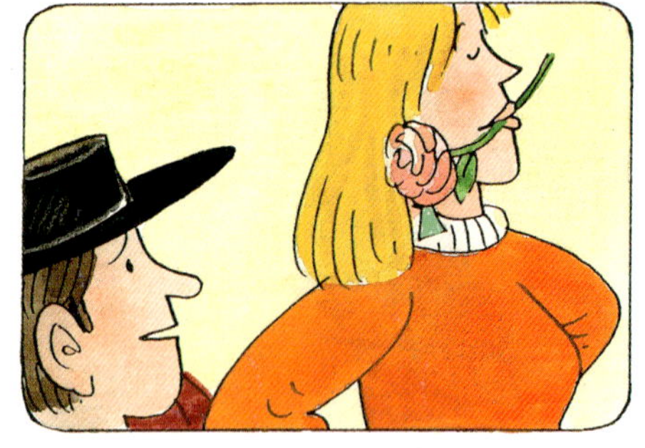

Kipper

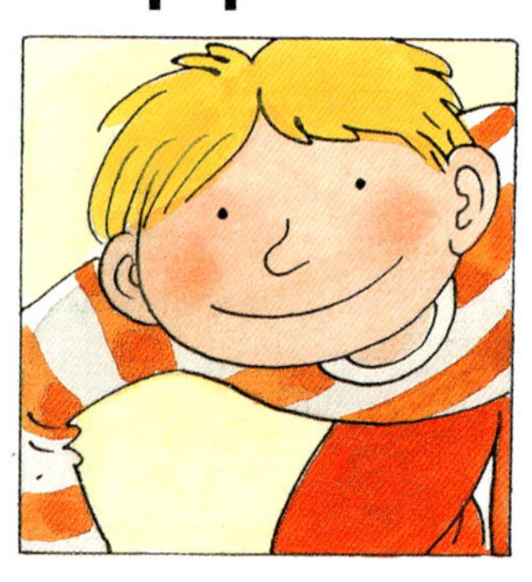

Floppy

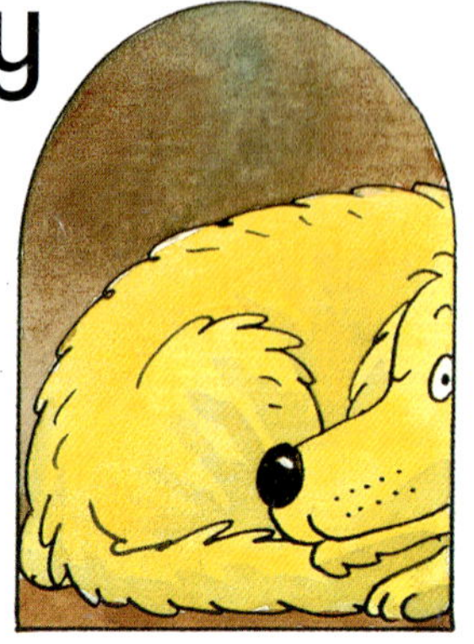

Biff and Chip

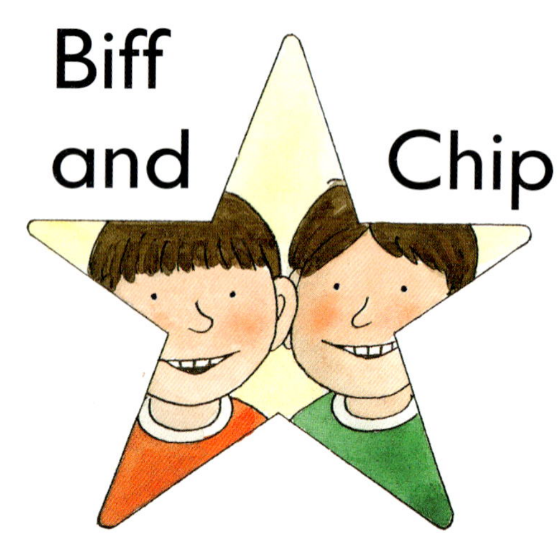